Passive Income

7 Predictable Ways to Generate a Passive Income Stream when you are over 40 and While Working a Full Time Job

Introduction

I want to thank you and congratulate you for downloading the book, *"Passive Income: 7 Predictable Ways to Generate a Passive Income Stream While Working a Full Time Job"*.

This book has actionable information on 7 predictable ways through which you can generate passive income while retaining your full-time job.

A passive income is any income earned from income streams that do not need consistent every day input. Traditionally, many used the term"passive income" in reference to income earned from investment vehicles such as stocks, dividends, rent, interest on monies, royalties, capital gains, etc. Thanks to technology, this definition has morphed.

Today, while the definition of a passive income still remains the same, income generated from sources that do not require consistent output, in light of a society entrenched in working a day job for 8 or more hours 5 days a week, any income generated from working 2-3 hours a day can fit into the passive income description.

Because of this and other reasons such as financial and time freedom, supplementation of income, unlimited income potential, and most importantly, being the 'boss,'creating a passive income stream to supplement, or even replace an active income has become the "it-thing" and thousands of people are now looking for ways to earn a passive income while working a day job.

Since you are reading this, undoubtedly, you would like to learn how to earn a passive income as a way to supplement your active income, or earn enough to leave the confines of your day job.

If this is what you desire, you're in luck because the internet has made the prospect easier and unlike days gone, to get started, you don't need thousands of dollars. All you need is a computer (or even a smartphone), and active internet connection, and 2-3 hours of your day for no less than 3 months. After this time (which is often how long it takes to setup an online-based, passive income-generating stream), you can work for as little as 4 hours a week and still earn well enough to quit your day job if you so wish.

In this book, we are going to discuss 7 highly potent, yet relatively easy to implement, online-based passive income streams you can implement while working a day job since they require minimal hours to setup (2-3 consistent hours per day).

The good thing about these passive income streams is that when you successfully implement one, you can move on to the others, and by so doing, create multiple passive income streams that take less than 4 hours per week to manage.

Thanks again for downloading this book. I hope you enjoy it!

Table of Contents

I won't go round in circles trying to justify why you should venture into passive income because given that you are reading this book, you perhaps have heard great things about passive income e.g. ease of scalability, the passive nature of the income, tax benefits etc., which has informed your decision to look out for ways to make passive income. Instead, we will immediately start by discussing the different strategies you can follow to make passive income in a step by step format.

1st Strategy: Blogging

Blogging is the most common and predictable way to earn a passive income. In fact, many of the other sources of online passive income anchor on blogs. In other words, if you have a blog that has a good enough readership, you can start and support almost all the other online passive income strategies that we will be discussing in this book.

Since you're not new to the internet, you have read success stories of bloggers such as Brett McKay of artofmanliness.com, John Chow of Johnchow.com, Mario Lavandeira of PerezHilton.com, and Pat Flynn of Smartpassiveincome.com, and other bloggers who earn thousands of dollars per month from blogging about topics and things they love. This goes to show you just how powerful blogging is as an income stream.

The good thing about blogging is that to get started, you need nothing but a passion, dedication (the willingness to dedicate 2-3 hours of your day to blogging), and a bit of easy to learn technical knowledge (which is where this book comes in). Here is how to go about it:

How to Start a Revenue-Generating Blog

In this guide, we are going to reveal how to use your free time (in the morning before heading to your day job or in the evening—morning works best because as Pat Flynn says, "always start your day by dedicating 2 hours to working for yourself) to create a blog that generates no less than $1,000 per month. Let's get to it:

Step 1: Choose a Topic/Niche

To set up a successful blog that earns you a passive income going into hundreds of thousands of dollars as you work your other job, sleep, or even travel, the first thing you need to do is choose a topic. Here, go with a topic that impassions you because at the end of the day, blogging should be fun and because it takes time to bear fruit—do not expect to make tons of money a month after starting—passion is a key ingredient because it ensures you stick to blogging when quitting seems like the best option.

With that said however, research from Wpromote shows that the top 5 most popular blog categories are music, fashion, travel, food, and beauty. While this also means these are the most competitive, you are free to go with what you feel most passionate about. At the end of the day, even if you chose a less competitive topic that does not impassion you, your chances of creating an income generating blog are very minimal since the prospect calls for patience and a lot of dedication. Once you have your topic of interest at hand...

Step 2: Choose a Domain and Hosting Option for Your Site

As indicated earlier, the greatest thing about blogging is that you do not need to invest anything other than your time; this is because if you choose to, you can use hosted blog option such as blogger.com, wordpress.com, or even squarespace.com. The downside to using these options is that while the hosting is free, the domain name is not brandable.

For instance, if you decide to create a blog about a specific genre of music such as reggae, and you choose to name your blog "one love reggae," if you go with the WordPress option, your domain name shall be "onelovereggae.wordpress.com. This, as you can see, is a mouthful. On the other hand, a self-hosted blog allows you to choose a brandable domain. Using the reggae example, the domain name would be onelovereggae.com. You can learn how to choose a domain name here.

A domain will cost you anywhere from $1-$15 per year while hosting will vary depending on the provider and the option you choose (BlueHost, iPage and HostGator have options starting from as little as $3 per month). This article has some great insight on how to settle on a hosting provider.

You shall also need to setup your blog and customize it as you see fit. Google these things—you will find tons of related information related to your chosen blogging platform. For instance, if you opt to use WordPress, the world's most popular blogging platform, you can get ideas on how to set up your WordPress blog from Siteground.com or WPbeginner.com.

Step 3: Start Writing and Driving Traffic to Your Blog

With your blog all set up, the next step is to start writing content. In the online space, content reigns supreme. This is because how unique, informational, and helpful to readers it is, and how well optimized it is for search bots will determine how popular your blog becomes and how much traffic it generates. More traffic equals more money potential.

When it comes to deciding what to blog about, your passion should come in handy and help you brainstorm topics. In terms of driving traffic to your blog, concentrate on being super helpful to readers by writing amazing content, and then optimize this content for search engines. This therefore means you have to conduct keyword research and use this to write for people and optimize your content for search. This is not as difficult as it sounds and with CMS (content management systems) such as WordPress, you will find tons of plugins (such as SEO Yoast) that shall help you with search engine optimization.

Another thing you should do here is create an editorial calendar so you avoid the mistake of blogging when you feel like it. Creating a revenue generating blog require consistency.

Brainstorm 50-100 blog ideas and spread them out on calendar (aim for a blog a day since research has shown that frequently updated blogs attract more traffic).

Step 4: Monetize

When your blog starts attracting visitors, you are free to monetize it by creating products related to your blog. For instance, if your blog is on reggae, you can create a reggae guitar guide for beginners eBook), affiliate marketing, or make money with advertisements from ad networks like Chitika, Media.net, , Ad Maven, Vibrant Media, Clicksor, Advertising.com, Google Adsense, , Revenue Hits, Revcontent, AdBlade, Undertone, , PropellerAds, WWW Promoter, Infolinks, Adbuff etc. or targeted ads from companies fit your audience. As I already mentioned, many of the other blog monetization options like selling software, mobile apps, selling physical products, independent publishing, membership sites, information courses etc. can be anchored on a blog so make sure to take blogging seriously if you really want to end up making real money from blogging. The opportunities for making passive income when you have a blog are endless! Monetization options for a traffic generating blog are endless and once you get consistent traffic, you will have your fair share of picks.

More important than monetizing is making sure the blog is helpful to readers and friendly to search engines.

As you shall note, the other strategies we shall discuss here shall depend on how well you can implement this one strategy because without a blog/website, the other strategies shall be less effective.

To help you out further, here are various resources related to creating an income-generating blog:

How to choose a niche for your blog

http://www.bloggingwizard.com

http://www.wpsuperstars.net

How to set up a WordPress blog
(WordPress is the easiest to use CMS)

http://www.wpbeginner.com

How to drive traffic to a blog

http://neilpatel.com

https://www.iwillteachyoutoberich.com

DOWNLOAD YOUR FREE BONUS:

5 PASSIVE INCOME BUSINESS MODELS VIDEO COURSE

Go to: http://quintons-school.teachable.com/

2nd Strategy: Affiliate Marketing

Affiliate marketing is an amazing way to generate a gushing stream of passive income. When well implemented, affiliate marketing can earn you hundreds of thousands of dollars per month, enough money to have you quit your day job and start doing whatever your heart desires.

Affiliate marketing is a business model where you "affiliate" yourself to products and services. In simple terms, this means you market other peoples' services and products and in exchange, whenever a customer you refer buys a product or service, you earn a percentage of the buying price. For instance, if you refer someone to a piece of software retailing for $500 and you have an affiliate relationship with the software company stipulating that for every referral, you will earn 20%, you will earn $100.

In the online space, the affiliate marketing business model uses special links called "affiliate links."Affiliate links are unique web links provided to affiliate marketers for marketing purposes. The link has a special cookie unique to you; the purpose of this cookie is to capture where the lead/referral is coming from so that when someone clicks on the link and buys something, the purchase reflects on your referral account and you can receive a commission for it.

Affiliate marketing offers exponential potential. For instance, if you have a popular reggae blog, you can affiliate yourself to reggae concerts sellers, guitar sellers, and other such companies that match your audience needs. You can do all this from the same website because to affiliate yourself, all you have to do is insert a link into a page or a post.

For instance, if you are writing a post title "10 amazing-sounding guitars ideal for reggae music," for each guitar on the list, you can drop an affiliate link to a retailer (make sure you have an affiliate relationship with the retailer), and when someone clicks on your affiliate link and makes a purchase, you shall earn a commission.

To get started on affiliate marketing, create a website or blog using the steps outlined in the previous strategy. Once the blog starts generating traffic on a consistent basis, decide which affiliate offers are a fit for your audience and affiliate yourself to these offers by inserting the affiliate links into your posts and pages. You don't have to have a personal relationship with the companies that are recruiting affiliates. You can register in affiliate marketplaces i.e. websites that help publishers find advertisers. Some of the popular places you can register as an affiliate include the following:

ClickBank

CJ Affiliate by Conversant (Formerly known as Commission Junction)

ShareASale

Amazon Associates

EBay Partner Network

Rakuten Affiliate Network

Avangate

Revenue Wire

TradeDoubler

And many others

In accordance with the law, every time you insert an affiliate link into your content or page, insert a disclaimer letting readers know that by using the affiliate link to make a purchase, you will earn a commission.

Another way to go about affiliate marketing is using paid advertising. For instance, let us assume you would like to affiliate yourself to a "custom guitar" service. You can use paid advertising on platforms such as Google AdWords and social media platforms such as Instagram, Facebook, Twitter, and other paid advertising options to promote the service to the masses.

To be successful at affiliate marketing, and therefore, earn a passive income even as you sleep, you are better off operating from a blog or website because this allows for centralization and diversification. For instance, even when you want to use paid advertising to promote a custom guitar service, you are likely to be more successful if you create a post reviewing the service (from a personal perspective), and then promoting this post on social media. This will ensure that when the service becomes popular, that one post can earn you thousands of dollars year after year without needing any maintenance.

As a rule of thumb, do not affiliate yourself to product or services you do not use because when you do and the service and products you promote fail to work as implied, your reputation will suffer because the internet hates fraudsters. To achieve massive success with affiliate marketing, place your offers at strategic areas of your website and pages.

Let us look at an example:

Assume you have a website that has 50 posts generating 1,000 views per month (total traffic=50,000). Out of this, assume that each page has affiliate offers from different companies offering a $100 product. If your conversation rate is 1% per month (a 1% conversion rate is very easy to achieve), it means out of your 50,000 visitors, 500 will be clicking on your affiliate links and purchasing. If your affiliate relationship with these providers stipulates that you earn 10% of the purchase price, each conversion shall earn you $10 and therefore, you shall earn more than $5, 000 each month.

The affiliate marketing process is as follows:

1. Drive massive amounts of traffic to your website.

2. Find affiliate programs and offers that fit your audience.

3. Insert your affiliate links into your wildly popular posts and pages while making sure that this insertion adds value to readers' lives.

4. Be open about your affiliate relationship by adding an affiliate disclaimer to each affiliate offer.

5. Optimize your conversion rate so you can convert as many of your web visitors as possible.

If you can do the above and find well-paying offers, you will be well on your way to earning money as you commute, travel, work at your day job, or even sleep. What a life!

Further reading

https://www.locationrebel.com

http://nichehacks.com

MonetizePros.com.

http://www.affiliatebible.com

http://www.wpeagle.com

Myworkfromhomemoney.com

NeilPatel.com

3rd Strategy: Membership Sites

A membership site is a blog-like website where members pay a monthly fee to access premium content not freely available on the blog section of the website.

Contrary to popular belief, creating a membership site does not require tons of technical knowledge such as web design or coding because with WordPress, you can use plugins to bar some information and make it available to paying members. One of the greatest things about a membership site is the recurrent nature of the business.

As an example, if the barred content you create for membership site is eBooks, podcasts, video and audio webinars, or virtual conferences, if you keep the information fresh and updated (for example, you offer webinars and conferences on a daily, weekly, or even monthly basis), if you keep the information valuable, paid members will keep paying the membership fee.

To get started, create a website/blog as indicated earlier. For this purpose, you can create WordPress based website (it's easier to manage thanks to plugins and an easy to use interface) and install a membership plugin such as MemberPress or S2member (simply search the plugin on the plugins search bar). The plugin shall guide you through the process of adding the product and payment options. Make sure this information is very relevant your web visitors and compels them to want to pay to join your membership site. Make sure that creating a username and password is easy and seamless too because if the process is not easy, users will be at odds and your conversion rate may suffer. You can also create various levels of membership options.

Creating a successful membership site depends on the following.

The first thing you have to do is build trust: no one wants to buy something from someone he or she does not know or trust. The best way to do this is to offer freebies such as trial or free content. For instance, assuming your website is on self-development, you can create free self-development content for your site as a way to build trust and show readers that if you have such valuable information on your free blog, the information restricted to members is infinitely better. This will make it easier for web visitors to subscribe to your membership and pay the monthly fee.

As obvious as it sounds, the key to success in this venture is to drive traffic to your site (traffic is central to all online-based, passive income strategies discussed here). To ensure you convert these visitors into paid members, create an effective lead magnet. A lead magnetis a bribe in the form of upgrades, freebies, and signup incentives that gets people to give you their contact information such as email and name. For instance, besides the free content, you can offer a free consultation.

Let us look at an example:

Assume you have a members only self-improvement blog where you have three levels: the free level, level one that offers premium content every month, level 2 that offers free content and 2 coaching sessions per month, and level 3 that offers weekly coaching sessions.

Assume that your site attracts 200,000 visitors per month. Out of these, 100,000 go for the free content. Out of the remaining 100,000, you convert 1% (1,000 people) as follows: 950 choose level 1 priced at $49 per month (total=$46,550), 30 choose level 2 priced at $99 per month (total=$2,970), and 20 choose level 3 priced at $299 per month (total=5,980), your total earning shall be $55, 500, which is not bad at all. Since the bulk of this revenue shall be from level 1 that does not require one on one consulting, you can use your weekend to create content for them.

As for the rest, you can schedule them into your calendar accordingly. If you give each of person a 30-minute consulting session and work for 2 hours every day (serving 4 people per day except on weekend), a month shall be enough time to offer premium one-on-one services that leave your client happy.

Once you reach such a point, you can take off the pressure by delegating tasks. For instance, you can outsource the creation of the premium content (after drafting it of course), uploading it to the site, customer service for member response, social media marketing and management, and simply concentrate on offering one on one coaching. This shall help you grow your business to a point where if you so want, you can quit your day job and concentrate on the membership site full time (thereby increasing your earning potential).

The beauty of membership sites is that they work across all niches and as long as people are interested in a specific topic and you can create highly valuable content on the same, you can earn money from it. For instance, you can create a membership site offering premium freelance writing jobs.

Further reading

http://theworldismyoffice.com

http://www.wpbeginner.com

https://www.inc.com

https://ontraport.com

4th Strategy: Kindle Publishing

Of the passive income strategies we shall discuss here, this is the only one that does not necessarily demand a website. And the good news about it is that you can make your first sale as a complete beginner within less than 24 hours!

Publishing books has always been profitable; so profitable in fact, that traditional publishers are constantly giving new writers book advances running into seven figures. The good news is that to create a publishing empire, you do not necessarily need to go the traditional publishing way especially considering that getting a publisher is not a stroll in the park. You can self-publish on Kindle.

Kindle publishing (Kindle Direct Publishing) is the publishing arm of technology giant Amazon. Launched in 2007, KDP as its abbreviated helps authors independently publish their book to Amazon's 193 million monthly visitors.

Kindle publishing, like affiliate marketing, offers unlimited potential especially if you are looking to publish more than one book (which you should if you want to earn thousands of dollars from the prospect). Here is everything you need to know about creating a passive income-generating kindle publishing empire:

Step 1: Choose a Niche

Your success as a Kindle publisher shall depend on your ability to find profitable niches topics on which to write books. The great thing here is that to do so, you need not look further than Amazon. No matter how great a writer you are, if you write a book on a topic that lacks readership, topic readers' want solutions to, you will be shooting yourself in the foot.

Here, the easiest thing you can do is think of a problem you would like to solve. Here is a secret no other passive income book shall tell you: ***if you are truly committed to creating lasting streams of passive income, you have to solve a problem people are willing to pay to solve***.

Once you have a problem in mind, visit the Kindle Best seller site. On the left hand side, you are going to see categories. Choose a category you think you can write a book on (or one that matches the problem you want to solve). If you are yet to decide which problem to tackle, simply choose a category you consider appealing.

When you navigate to a specific category, you will head deeper into that category and you may find other sub-categories. For instance, if you decide to go with self-help, under it, you will see other sub-categories such as creativity, eating disorders, happiness, etc. Choose one you want to scrutinize further and keep digging until you get to the sub niches.

As an example, below are the top 100 books in the niche self-help and sub-niche eating disorder and body image. Once you're in the bestseller niche and sub-niche, look for patterns. Can you notice 2 or more books on related topics? If you notice 2 or more books on a related topic, this is an indicator that this topic is popular and doing well.

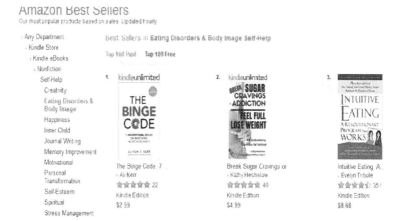

The next step is to dig further. Amazon Kindle ranks books according to their download and reviews. A popular and often downloaded book will have a higher rank with 1 being the most downloaded book.

When you notice related books, click on each book (you can open different tabs on your browser), and then scroll down; you will see the book rank. For instance, from the above, we see that binge eating is a popular topic because at the time of writing this, the 1st book (Binge eating code), the 4th book (brain over binge), and several other books (3rd, 9th, 13th, 14th, and several others) are on the list of 100.

The next step is to open some of these books to see their rank. At the time of writing this, Binge eating code ranks at 14, 477 in the entire Kindle store. Intuitive eating ranks at 17, 374, and Brain over Binge ranks at 18,168 respectively. This rank changes every minute (Amazon updates it every 6 hours).

Product details

File Size: 3740 KB
Print Length: 188 pages
Page Numbers Source ISBN: 1999786408
Simultaneous Device Usage: Unlimited
Publisher: MindFree; 1 edition (July 6, 2017)
Publication Date: July 6, 2017
Sold by: Amazon Digital Services LLC
Language: English
ASIN: B073HDB6ZN
Text-to-Speech: Enabled
X-Ray: Not Enabled
Word Wise: Enabled
Lending: Not Enabled
Enhanced Typesetting: Not Enabled
Amazon Best Sellers Rank: #14,477 Paid in Kindle Store (See Top 100 Paid in Kindle Store)

> #1 in Kindle Store > Kindle eBooks > Nonfiction > Self-Help > **Eating Disorders & Body Image**
> #9 in Books > Health, Fitness & Dieting > Mental Health > **Eating Disorders**
> #36 in Kindle Store > Kindle eBooks > Health, Fitness & Dieting > Diets & Weight Loss > Diets > **Weight Maintenance**

Product details

File Size: 3297 KB
Print Length: 369 pages
Page Numbers Source ISBN: 1250004047
Publisher: St. Martin's Griffin; 3 edition (August 7, 2012)
Publication Date: August 7, 2012
Sold by: Amazon Digital Services LLC
Language: English
ASIN: B006ZL3P4G
Text-to-Speech: Enabled
X-Ray: Enabled
Word Wise: Enabled
Lending: Not Enabled
Screen Reader: Supported
Enhanced Typesetting: Enabled
Amazon Best Sellers Rank: #17,374 Paid in Kindle Store (See Top 100 Paid in Kindle Store)

> #3 in Kindle Store > Kindle eBooks > Nonfiction > Self-Help > **Eating Disorders & Body Image**
> #5 in Kindle Store > Kindle eBooks > Medical eBooks > Special Topics > **Nutrition**
> #13 in Books > Health, Fitness & Dieting > Mental Health > **Eating Disorders**

Product details

File Size: 1215 KB
Print Length: 328 pages
Publisher: Camellia Publishing (January 1, 2011)
Publication Date: January 1, 2011
Sold by: Amazon Digital Services LLC
Language: English
ASIN: B005F9UZ1U
Text-to-Speech: Enabled
X-Ray: Enabled
Word Wise: Enabled
Lending: Not Enabled
Screen Reader: Supported
Enhanced Typesetting: Enabled
Amazon Best Sellers Rank: #18,168 Paid in Kindle Store (See Top 100 Paid in Kindle Store)
#4 in Kindle Store > Kindle eBooks > Nonfiction > Self-Help > **Eating Disorders & Body Image**
#15 in Books > Health, Fitness & Dieting > Mental Health > **Eating Disorders**
#214 in Kindle Store > Kindle eBooks > Biographies & Memoirs > **Memoirs**

The idea here is to look for related books that are ranking well. If several related books rank at 1>20,000, this is a niche worth pursuing; it means the book ranking at 20,000 is selling a minimum of 3-15 books per day. The screenshot below shows the Kindle rank in relation to book sales and potential incomes.

- ✓ Rank 50,000 to 100,000— selling 0— 1 book a day.

- ✓ Rank 10,000 to 50,000— selling 3 to 15 books a day.

- ✓ **Rank 5,500 to 10,000— selling 15 to 30 books a day.**

- ✓ Rank 3,000 to 5,500— selling 30 to 50 books a day.

- ✓ *Rank 500 to 3,000— selling 50 to 200 books a day*

- ✓ Rank 350 to 500— selling 200 to 300 books a day.

- ✓ Rank 100 to 350— selling 300 to 500 books a day.

- ✓ Rank 35 to 100— selling 500 to 1,000 books a day.

- ✓ Rank 10 to 35— selling 1,000 to 2,000 books a day.

- ✓ Rank of 5 to 10— selling 2,000 to 4,000 books a day.

- ✓ Rank of 1 to 5— selling 4,000 + books a day.

Once you find a niche, you have to come up with a title and subtitle for your book and then brainstorm and mindmap your ideas for the book. Fully flesh the mind map until you have a table of content like structure for your book.

Step 2: Write the Book, Create Cover, and Publish

With your mind map at hand, you will notice that your book will most likely write itself and from there, you can dedicate yourself to writing 1,000 words of your book per day. In about 10 days, you will have a publish-worthy book. Once done with the first draft, edit the book a first, second, and third time; if possible, hire an editor. Talking about hiring someone to write your book:

The most amazing thing about the Kindle publishing strategy is that even if you are not the creative type, you can hire someone to write the book for you. You will find great freelancers on site such as Upwork.com, Freelancer.com, WriteArticlesForMe.com, EpicWrite.com, TheWritingSummit.com and other platforms.

Once the book is ready, hire someone to create a book cover on Fiverr.com (or do it yourself if you have the expertise), sign up for Kindle Publishing, and follow the prompts to publish your book.

Step 3: Market the Book

Like most passive income businesses, how much you end up earning from Kindle publishing will depend on how much traffic you can drive to your book. The more exposure your book gets, the better it is likely to perform and the more revenue you are bound to generate.

To market your book, you can use options such as social media, free and paid book promos, paid advertising, guest blogging, and other such ideas.

Let us look at an example:

Assume you create 5 great books that rank at 10,000. This means you shall be selling 15 books of each title each day. Depending on your price point (how you price the book—go for nothing below $2.99 so you can take 70% of the revenue share), you shall be earning $156.957 from the five books per day (70/100 X $ 2.99= $2.093 X 15 books sold each day X 5 book titles= $156.957 per day). This therefore means on a good month, you can take home $4000+. This is not bad considering the effort and the fact that after publishing the book, marketing it will require less than 30 minutes per day.

Further reading

https://kindlepreneur.com

http://okdork.com

https://www.tckpublishing.com

https://www.thecreativepenn.com

DOWNLOAD YOUR FREE BONUS:

5 PASSIVE INCOME BUSINESS MODELS VIDEO COURSE

Go to: http://quintons-school.teachable.com/

5th Strategy: YouTube Videos

Never before has man loved video than he does now. Today, videos are the most consumed form of online content. From funny cat videos, to game walkthroughs, to makeup videos, video is the "it-thing." And in the world of video, nothing beats YouTube.

Owned by Google, and boasting of over 30 million visitors per day, YouTube is a prime way to generate a passive income. How do you go about this? What do you need to do to become a YouTube millionaire? Let us discuss this:

Step 1: Setup Your Account and Start Creating Content

This one is very straightforward: create an account on YouTube. The process is very straightforward, as all you need is a Google Account. As you do so, however, you may want to pay attention to the nature of your YouTube channel (the topics you shall be covering) and if possible, have the name reflect on the title of your channel. For instance, if you intend to create videos that motivate people, you could name your channel something along the lines of "dailymotivation."

When thinking about which types of videos to create, remember to follow your passion or ask yourself a question such as "what do I know and can teach easily?" This will help you come up with an idea for a channel. The idea here is simple: come up with a channel people will find helpful; this does not necessarily mean that the channel and the videos you create have to be educational. Always remember that if people are actively searching for specific information, you can create video content for it irrespective of whether what they are searching for is funny videos or even weird videos.

When you start creating content, make sure the content is valuable enough to attract views and shares. As an example, the world seems to like videos of "unboxing/reviewing products." If you can buy niche products (products such as vapes), unbox them, and then show people how to use them, you have something on your hands, provided the videos you create are clear and helpful. The good thing about creating YouTube videos is that if you cannot afford expensive shooting cameras, you can get started with the camera on your high-end smartphone.

Step 2: Drive Traffic to the Channel/Video

After creating 10 or 20 videos and uploading them to your channel (do this immediately after creating your channel and before you start promoting it), hit the road and start marketing your channel and the specific videos you have created. The best way to do this is to share the videos on social media (you can even use paid advertising to promote the video to its relevant target audience), or share the video on your blog (see how they two relate?).

The following resources shall teach you optimize your channel for search as well as how to promote your YouTube channel:

https://blog.hootsuite.com

https://www.outbrain.com

Step 3: Monetize

After building your fan and subscriber base and reached 10,000 per video, add monetization to your channel to start making money. Monetizing YouTube is relatively easy because all you have to do is allow Google to serve ads on your channel/videos (the material has to be non-copyrighted).

The monetization option is on your YouTube sidebar on the channel, status, and features option (you have to be logged is as a YouTube publisher). From here, simply enable monetization.

Once you have this setup, you are ready to start earning from YouTube. Let us look at an example:

YouTube pays through Google AdSense through a CPM (cost per Mille or cost per thousand). This means they pay for every 1,000-ad impressions. The CPM for each impression may be $0.1 to $10 depending on the niche you are serving.

Here is how the math would look if we go with a $0.1 CPM:

1,000 views=$0.1

10,000 views=$1

100,000 views=$10

1,000,000 views=$100

10,000,000 views=$1,000

100,000,000 views=$10,000

1,000,000,000 views=$100,000

As you can see, how much you end up earning from YouTube will depend on your ad impression, which shall depend on how many views you can drive to your website; therefore, the more traffic you drive to your channel and videos, the higher the earning potential.

One of the greatest thing about YouTube is that once the video is live and generating views, the multiplication factor is great and in most instances, the video shall market itself (especially if it's good) through person-to-person sharing and social shares:

Further reading

https://www.quora.com

https://www.entrepreneur.com

https://creatoracademy.youtube.com

https://monetizepros.com

https://www.incomediary.com

DOWNLOAD YOUR FREE BONUS:

5 PASSIVE INCOME BUSINESS MODELS VIDEO COURSE

Go to: http://quintons-school.teachable.com/

6th Strategy: Ecommerce Site

One thing we know for sure is that how we shop has changed. Today, many of us would rather shop online. This has precipitated the rise of ecommerce moguls who are earning millions of dollars per month. Here, think along the lines of Amazon, Alibaba, eBay, Etsy, Baidu, and other similar ones.

You too can start such a business without having to give up your day job. Here is how:

Step 1: Decide What to Sell

The prospect of creating a successful ecommerce site hinges on having something to sell; without a product, getting started will not be easy. This pays credence to the importance of having a great product to sell.

The best way to go about deciding what to sell is to create something that solves a problem (solving a problem is central to online success) or take something in existence, make it better and then market it better. The second option is easier if you are not a creator.

When choosing a product, pay attention to niches you find familiar and are passionate about because selling something you are not familiar with means you will waste a lot of time trying to figure out how to connect with, or sell to the target audience. When you restrict yourself to a niche you are familiar with, you make this process much easier.Amazon is a great place to look for niche ideas for ecommerce sites.

The following resources should help you with finding the perfect products for your ecommerce store:

https://www.shopify.com

https://www.shopify.com

https://www.bigcommerce.com

https://www.ecomdash.com

Step 2: Source the Product

Those already making money in the ecommerce scene will willingly tell you that Alibaba is the best place to source for products. To use Alibaba, all you have to do is head to the site, type in the main keywords for the product you chose, and choose manufacturers who meet your specific criteria. As a rule, go with gold suppliers.

Step 3: Set up Your Store and Start Selling

Once you have a supplier for your product, the next step is to create your store. Here, you can create a store on sites such as Amazon, Etsy, eBay or Shopify, or create your own ecommerce website. Here, if you know nothing about ecommerce, you can recruit a capable web designer on sites such as Upwork.com or Freelancer.com and others.

After setting up your site, start uploading content descriptions for your merchandise and selling. To sell, however,

Step 4: Drive Traffic to Your Site

To drive traffic to you ecommerce site, you can use paid advertising (as long as the return on investment is ok), or seek organic traffic by performing SEO on the site content.

As an example, if you create a store than offers 5 products priced at $20, of which you 100 products per month per product, if the initial cost of creating and shipping the product is $10, it means in a month, your gross profit could be $5,000, give or take. This is without having to work tons of hours to generate the same.

Further Reading

https://ecommerce-platforms.com

http://www.huffingtonpost.com

https://www.shopify.com

https://www.oberlo.com

https://www.shopify.com

7th Strategy: Service Arbitrage Business

The other way you can generate a passive income is by selling other people's service, i.e. you act as a paid intermediary between those seeking services and those selling them. The best example of such sites is most freelancing websites such as Upwork.com, Fiverr.com, iWriter.com, Freelancer.com and the likes.

The idea behind this is relatively simple: find people looking to offer specific services online, services such as writing, find clients willing to pay for the same services at a rate higher than the one asked by the service provider, connect the two (preferably through a web portal) and pocket the difference.

Getting started on this business model is easy and very straightforward: all you need is to choose the service you want to arbitrage. This could be a service such as SEO analysis, book covers, social media management and marketing, etc. Once you have this core service in mind, start looking for service providers offering such services. You can find many of these on freelancing sites and then foster a relationship with them.

The next step is to search for clients looking for people seeking these services, offer to provide the services at a rate higher than what you shall offer the service provider and voila, you are in business. The greatest thing about this is that it does not require much time or much from you in terms of monetary investment.

For instance, if you decide to arbitrage "SEO analysis services," you can find a great service provider who is willing to offer amazing SEO services at $1,000 and on the other hand, a company that is willing to pay someone $1,500 for the same service. If you sell yourself as a great service provider for this company, and if the person you hire does an amazing job, you can earn $500 from being an intermediary.

The down side to this type of business is that it will take a substantial amount of time to create a convincing profile for the specific service you are offering. However, if you are good at this, which you can manage—creating trust and credibility—by creating an amazing portfolio site for the specific service you are arbitraging, you can be well on your way to earning thousands of dollars per week.

For instance, assume that it takes you about 6 months to create a great portfolio site for SEO analysis service and that on a weekly basis, 3 web owners reach out for your services (because you have already established yourself as an authority on the subject) paying $1500 each. If you outsource the same service to your capable service provider for $1,000, you can pocket the difference, which is $1,500 for the three clients. If this holds week-in-week-out, you can earn $4,500 with the potential to earn so much more as your business grows.

The most amazing thing about service arbitrage is that it is labor free: all you have to do is find service providers, find companies seeking the services offered by these service providers, offer the services and once the contract is yours, simply offer it to the service provider at a lesser fee. While it sounds fraudulent, there is nothing fraudulent about it just as there is nothing wrong about retail arbitrage.

Further reading

https://www.entrepreneurs-journey.com

https://www.warriorforum.com

DOWNLOAD YOUR FREE BONUS:

5 PASSIVE INCOME BUSINESS MODELS VIDEO COURSE

Go to: http://quintons-school.teachable.com/

Conclusion

We have come to the end of the book. Thank you for reading and congratulations for reading until the end.

This book has shown you 7 ways to create a passive income online. Implement these ways one after the other (setting up most requires less than 3 hours of work per day, which you can do before or after work), and in 6 months to 1 year, your business should be at a point where it earns you a steady income without the need for every day work.

When you get to that point, you shall be financially free and stable.

If you found the book valuable, can you recommend it to others? One way to do that is to post a review on Amazon.

Click here to leave a review for this book on Amazon!

Thank you and good luck!

DOWNLOAD YOUR FREE BONUS:

5 PASSIVE INCOME BUSINESS MODELS VIDEO COURSE

Go to: http://quintons-school.teachable.com/

I need your help......

Thank you for purchasing and reading this book, I sincerely hope that you find value in the techniques and implement them into your life.

I created this book to help people start the journey of creating and building passive income streams. My goal is to let people know what options are available to them so that they can take advantage of them.

If you did find value in the book please take a minute to review the book and give your feedback as to what was good about and where it could improve.

This will help me in 2 ways:

1. It will help people decide if this book is worth buying.

2. Your feedback will help me make changes and improve the book.

Made in the USA
Middletown, DE
02 March 2018